THE NEED TO KNOW LIBRARY™

EVERYTHING YOU NEED TO KNOW ABOUT
HATE CRIMES

DANICA DAVIDSON

Rosen
YA™
New York

Published in 2018 by The Rosen Publishing Group, Inc.
29 East 21st Street, New York, NY 10010

Library of Congress Cataloging-in-Publication Data

Names: Davidson, Danica author.
Title: Everything you need to know about hate crimes / Danica Davidson.
Description: New York : Rosen Publishing, 2018. | Series: The need to know library | Includes bibliographical references and index. | Audience: Grades 7–12.
Identifiers: LCCN 2017019684| ISBN 9781508176688 (library bound) | ISBN 9781508176671 (pbk.) | ISBN 9781508176701 (6 pack)
Subjects: LCSH: Hate crimes—United States—Juvenile literature.
Classification: LCC HV6773.52 D39 2018 | DDC 364.150973—dc23
LC record available at https://lccn.loc.gov/2017019684

Manufactured in the United States of America

CONTENTS

INTRODUCTION

With the media reporting on hate crimes, many young people can feel scared and uncertain, and worry they might be victims. People are chosen as victims of hate crimes simply because of who they are or even whom they are perceived to be, whether it is based on their culture, religion, gender, sexual orientation, or another aspect of them, which can make hate crimes especially unsettling.

Hate crimes are also part of a bigger framework because an attack against an individual in a hate crime feels like an attack on the whole group. Attacks against individual people, left unchecked, can lead to further attacks, causing fear in entire communities. Crimes like genocide, or trying to erase an entire group of people, are extreme examples of hate crimes.

Hate crime laws and facts might look simple on the surface, but the whole subject is actually very complex. Looking through human history, we see there are many instances of love in the world, but there are many instances of hate, too. Hate crime laws are just a newer way of dealing with criminal activity based on bias for an individual or group, but they are dealing with issues that have lasted as long as recorded history.

Statistically, most people will not be the victim of a hate crime, but that doesn't mean hate crimes or hate won't affect them. There are still many myths and misconceptions out there about hate crimes, and people

Forty-nine people were killed and fifty-eight were wounded by Omar Mateen, an ISIS supporter who attacked people at the Pulse nightclub for being gay in 2016.

have differing opinions on the best way to fight hatred. All of this can feel overwhelming, and hate crime laws can be a difficult, touchy subject. But the first step when tackling an issue like hate is knowledge—to learn why hate exists, how it manifests, and what have been found to be the best ways to prevent it. The following sections provide an overview on hate crimes, discussing what does and doesn't count as a hate crime, what the laws are around them, and which people are most likely to be victims and perpetrators. With this knowledge, young people can better understand the situation and feel empowered to help create a world without so much hate.

CHAPTER ONE

WHAT IS A HATE CRIME?

On June 17, 2015, members of the predominantly black Emanuel African Methodist Episcopal Church were meeting for a Bible study when they were joined by Dylann Roof, a twenty-one-year-old white supremacist who wanted to start a race war. Roof maintained a website that spoke about his loathing of blacks, Hispanics, and Jews, and he had decided to go beyond talk. After about an hour, he pulled a gun on the parishioners, killing nine. According to authorities, he said, "You all are taking over our country. Y'all want something to pray about? I'll give you something to pray about."

Roof was later arrested, charged, and found guilty of thirty-three counts of federal hate crimes. The hate crime charges were filed since Roof had sought out his victims specifically because they were black. He was condemned by people internationally, but he also became a hero in circles where people shared his racist ideology, and some people in those circles wanted to follow his lead. In February 2017, the FBI worked to arrest twenty-nine-year-old Benjamin

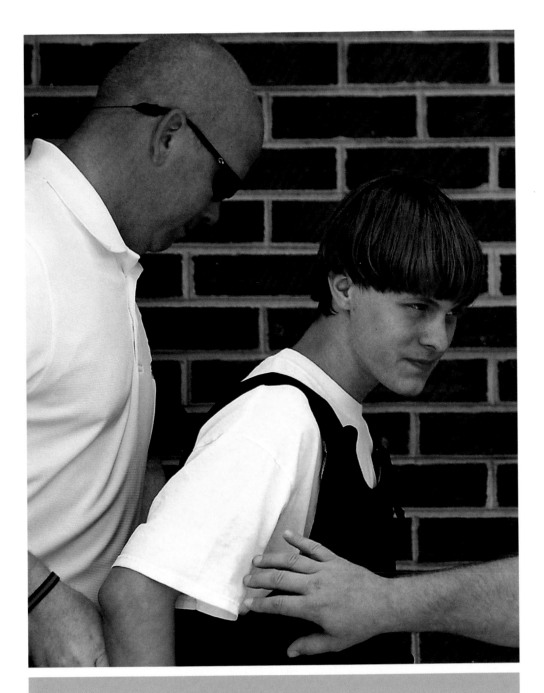

Then-suspect Dylann Roof is seen here in police custody on June 18, 2015, one day after committing his murder spree.

Thomas Samuel McDowell, saying he was a white supremacist who planned to attack a synagogue "in the spirit of Dylann Roof."

The Emanuel African Methodist Episcopal Chuch attack became a symbol of hate crimes, but there is no way to sum up all hate crimes into one incident. The church attack was more extreme than the majority of hate crimes committed, and it is far from the only hate crime out there. Each year thousands of hate crimes occur in the United States and most are not covered by the news and do not involve murder, but they are used to terrorize communities. So what is a hate crime, how does it work, and who are the people most likely involved?

HISTORY OF THE TERM

The term "genocide" was created toward the end of World War II to describe what happened in the Holocaust. Something similar happened with hate crimes. Journalists, politicians, and activists were noting how people were being illegally attacked or harassed based on who they were. Property owned by minorities was being destroyed. There was no term to describe these events. This is how the term "hate crime" got started in the 1980s. While there were technically some laws involving hate crimes before then, giving this issue a name helped differentiate these crimes from other violent crimes that have different motives.

Over the years, more groups have been added to the official description, causing more people to be protected by these laws. The FBI, which has been tracking and compiling information on hate crimes since the early 1990s, defines a hate crime as "a criminal offense committed against a person, property, or society that is motivated, in whole or in part, by the offender's bias against a race, religion, disability, sexual orientation, or ethnicity/national origin."

In other words, if a person breaks the law to attack another person or property simply because he or she doesn't like the person's race, religion, disability, sexual orientation, or ethnicity/national origin, that counts as a hate crime. If a person attacks someone of a different race or religion, or one of the other categories, but that is not the reason or one of the reasons for the attack, then it is not a hate crime.

A person might also commit a crime against some- one they perceive to be part of a group they don't like. Even if the victim does not turn out to be part of that group, it counts as a hate crime because the crime wouldn't have been committed against that person otherwise. An example of this was the attack on a Sikh temple in Wisconsin in 2012, where the perpetrator, a man with neo-Nazi beliefs, seemed to think he was attacking Muslims. Six people were killed before the gunman committed suicide. Mistaking Sikhs for another group did not make it count as any less of a hate crime, and this is far from the only example of something like this happening.

This does not mean that all acts of hate count as hate crimes. For example, a person could pass out flyers with hate speech on them, but because they are protected by free speech in the First Amendment, it would be called a "bias incident" or "hate incident" and not a hate crime. The person would not get into legal trouble. Likewise, a person can say or believe things other people might find prejudicial, and this is protected as free speech. The racist website belonging to Dylann Roof was used as further evidence that what he committed was a hate crime, but the words themselves did not come with penalties, and if he hadn't committed a violent crime, his website wouldn't have been an issue. A person could get in trouble for violently threatening another person, but that's because threatening someone that way is already illegal.

When a black church in South Carolina burned in 2015, many suspected arson as the cause. This fire was later proven to be caused by a lightning strike.

WHAT COUNTS AS A HATE CRIME?

A hate crime can be anything from intimidation (purposefully scaring a person) to murder. Other well-known types of hate crimes include physical and sexual assault. According to hate crime laws, it's the motive that matters.

A hate crime can also be done against property, like attacking a religious or cultural center solely out of hatred for people of that religion or culture. Sometimes, people find their homes vandalized with hateful slurs or hate symbolism.

LEO FRANK

In 1913, Leo Frank was a Jewish businessman in Atlanta who was convicted of raping and murdering a thirteen-year-old Christian girl named Mary Phagan, despite a lack of evidence. Nazism was soon to rise in Europe, and anti-Semitism (hatred of Jews) was also common in the United States. During Frank's trial, people chanted, "Hang the Jew, or we'll hang you!" The prosecutors used Frank's Jewishness against him, implying that because he was Jewish, something was wrong with him. Because of doubts about his guilt, the governor waived Frank's original death sentence. In response, a mob broke into Frank's prison, kidnapped him, and lynched him. Community leaders were among those in the lynching party, and more than a thousand people came to witness the lynching, but no one was ever tried for it. *The New York Times* noted, "Lynching mobs are usually composed of riff-raff, but this one consisted or leading citizens of the community, men prominent in business and social circles." Frank's death led to a renewed rise in the hate group the Klu Klux Klan and gave more impetus to the newly started Anti-Defamation League (ADL), a nonprofit that fights hate against Jews and other groups. It was only after Frank's death that the state of Georgia pardoned him, saying he did not actually commit the crime that had him imprisoned and killed. More than one hundred years later, some hate groups continue to insist that Frank was guilty and use it as a way to stir up anti-Jewish sentiment. While this happened before the term "hate crime" existed, it helped pave the way to our understanding of hate crimes today. Meanwhile, Phagan's murder remains officially unsolved.

WHAT PURPOSE DO HATE CRIMES SERVE?

A hate crime can be a way to put fear into an entire community. As an example, if a Native American is targeted and attacked because of the fact that he or she is Native American, it can lead other Native Americans to feel threatened. This remains true for any group. Marginalized groups that have experienced genocide or second-class citizenship can feel especially threatened when there is a hate crime in their midst because it reminds them of what has happened before and what could happen again.

A lithograph recalls the Cherokee being made to leave their native land in the 1830s, a forced march and relocation that happened to different Native American tribes.

Because of this, a hate crime has been described as an individual act of terrorism. It generally does not have the same massive scope as many acts of terrorism, but there are overlaps and it puts the same fear in people.

But sometimes hate crimes are committed by people who find the idea of them to be exciting, or because they believe that they are threatened by another group, even if they are not. According to the National Institute of Justice, just 1 percent of hate crime perpetrators feel "so strongly committed to bigotry that they make hate a career."

MYTHS AND FACTS

MYTH: There's no such thing as a hate crime.

FACT: Some politicians and activists dismiss the entire idea of hate crimes and try to pass them off as hoaxes. Whatever a person's personal opinion on hate crime legislation, it is the law of the land, and it therefore exists. Moving aside from the law angle, there's still the matter that it's easy to prove that sometimes a person attacks or commits a crime against another person solely because of a group that person belong to, and that's why it's differentiated from other crimes. As with any other crime, there will be examples of some people making false claims, but the majority of people reporting hate crimes are shown to be telling the truth.

MYTH: Hate crime laws fix everything.

FACT: There is no single way to fight violent hateful actions. Many proponents of hate crime legislation also work on issues of bias and tolerance, going to the root of the issue. Hate crime legislation is used to punish perpetrators and to send a message that this sort of hateful crimes will not be tolerated. A person might be less likely to commit a hate crime if he or she knows there's a law in place, but most supporters of hate crime legislation would agree they don't want to rest their laurels on hate crime laws alone.

MYTH: If someone posts something about hate crimes online, it has to be true.

FACT: In part because hate crimes can be controversial, there is a lot of misinformation out there. Sometimes, people are unaware of what they're talking about, or they can purposefully mislead. When researching hate crime information online, check the sources. For instance, are they sourced by the FBI or by a blog anyone could put up? It'd also be useful to research in multiple places, because then you're less likely to be in what's called an "echo chamber," where the website repeats what a person wants to hear as opposed to proven facts.

CHAPTER TWO

WHO ARE THE MOST LIKELY VICTIMS OF HATE CRIMES?

Because of the nature of hate crimes, anyone can potentially be a victim or perpetrator, no matter what group he or she belongs to. Some groups are more likely to experience hate crimes than others, as the following breakdown of those numbers in the United States show. Unless otherwise stated, all these statistics come from the FBI.

RACE-BASED HATE CRIMES

While numbers vary each year, the most common type of hate crime in America is based on race. Within the racial category, African Americans have the highest number of hate crimes committed against them. In 2010, 70 percent of race-based victims were African American, and in 2015, it was 52.2 percent. Incidents of racism against blacks in America is easily traced back to a history of slavery and institutional racism, like being treated differently by the court system. Before and during the civil rights movement, it was not uncommon

On August 28, 1963, the March on Washington for Jobs and Freedom took place, which included Martin Luther King's "I Have a Dream" speech. Here, marchers show their demands.

for a black person to be attacked or killed for being black. This still goes on today, though not with the same numbers as in the past.

In the category of racially based hate crimes, white people have the second highest number of attacks done against them. In 2010, 17.7 percent of racially based hate crimes were against white people, and in 2015, it was 18.7 percent. This goes against a commonly held but inaccurate belief that white people can only be perpetrators of hate crimes, not victims.

After this, the next groups with the highest numbers are Hispanics, Native Americans, and Asians, all of whom have experienced prejudice and oppression in the United States. According to the Southern Poverty Law Center, "Violence against American Indians, much of it motivated by racial hatred, is a pervasive yet obscure problem that is especially prevalent in so-called 'border towns'—majority white cities abutting reservations—where cultures clash against the historical backdrop of institutionalized racism, cultural subjugation, and genocide." While attacks against Native Americans are lower in numbers than for some other groups, the fact that there are so few Native Americans makes it an especially prevalent problem, because per capita Native Americans face especially high numbers of attacks.

After the Los Angeles County Commission on Human Relations noted that hate crimes against Asians rose three times in Los Angeles County from 2014 and 2015, the foundation Asian Americans Advancing Justice started a special tracker for hate crimes against Asian Americans and Pacific Islanders. When looking at the chart for hate crimes against ethnicities, the majority of the crimes are directed toward Hispanic people and are often tied with anti-immigration rhetoric, even if the victim is an American citizen.

RELIGION-BASED HATE CRIMES

Each year, Jewish people dominate this chart with the most hate crimes committed against them.

16TH STREET CHURCH BOMBING

During the civil rights movement, Klansmen set up a bomb in the 16th Street Baptist Church, an African American church in Birmingham, Alabama. When the bomb went off, it killed four girls under the age of fifteen: Addie Mae Collins, Denise McNair, Carole Robertson, and Cynthia Wesley. More people were hurt in the bomb and the riots that took place afterward. The next day, President John F. Kennedy and Dr. Martin Luther King Jr. spoke out about the bombing, condemning it. The Klan had chosen to bomb this site in an attempt to scare people and put a stop to the civil rights movement. Instead, the act was widely criticized and got people more involved in civil rights. Like the Leo Frank case, this occurred before the term "hate crime" existed, but it helped change America's understanding of hate and hate-based crimes. The bombing helped the passing of the Civil Rights Act in 1964. Years would pass before members of the Klan were arrested and successfully tried and convicted for the bombing.

Sometimes, the percentage of hate crimes against Jews rises to about 70 percent, even though Jews make up only about 2 percent of the American population. This is a continuation of what has been called "the world's oldest hatred," which has included centuries of persecutions and killings.

Religion-based hate crimes can especially target people whose religion is made obvious by their clothing, like Muslim women in head scarves or Sikhs in turbans.

Muslims are the second most likely group to experience religion-based hate crimes, and this number has risen since the September 11, 2001, terror attacks, though it doesn't come near the number of anti-Jewish attacks. Oftentimes, these anti-Muslim attacks are speared by a false belief that all Muslims are terrorists or otherwise dangerous. In addition to targeting Muslims, sometimes anti-Muslim attacks go after people deemed to "look Muslim," like Indians, Sikhs, and Middle Easterners. Other religious groups that experience hate crimes include Catholics,

Eastern Orthodox Church members, Protestants, Sikhs, and Hindus, among others.

SEXUAL ORIENTATION–BASED HATE CRIMES

Sexual orientation is another common cause of hate crime, especially against gay men, who are victims of more than half the crimes in this category. Lesbians also have a high percentage of hate crimes directed at them. Lower on the list are bisexual and heterosexual people, who typically each experience less than 3 percent of hate crimes in this category. In 2015, about 20 percent "were victims of antilesbian, gay, bisexual, or transgender (mixed group) bias."

GENDER-BASED AND GENDER IDENTITY–BASED HATE CRIMES

One of the increasingly more common categories of hate crimes is based on gender or gender identity. Men, women, and gender-nonconforming individuals are sought out and attacked, sometimes killed, in this type of hate crime.

In 2015, the FBI reported seventy-six incidents of this type of hate crime, which might seem insignificant. But the number has been increasing as more people come out as transgender.

After Islan Nettles was beaten to death for being transgender, a vigil was held on August 27, 2013, in Harlem, New York City. Then-mayoral candidate Bill de Blasio (*left background*) attended.

DISABILITIES-BASED HATE CRIMES

Hate crimes against disabled people are not reported as much as some other types of hate crimes. In 2015, there were eighty-eight hate crimes reported involving either physical or mental disability. However, it can be difficult to find exact numbers because the victim may not be able to tell or may have to depend on another person to report it for him or her.

In January 2017, hate crime charges were filed against four black people who harassed and physically

BRANDON TEENA

In 1993, Brandon Teena was a twenty-one-year-old transgender man who was raped and killed. John Lotter and Marvin "Tom" Nissen, two friends of Teena's girlfriend, took issue with Teena's gender identity and became violent. First they sought out to shame him by taking his clothes off, and they later raped him. Had their victim not been transgender, they wouldn't have done this, which is what makes it considered a hate crime. Teena reported the assault to police, but the police officer seemed more interested in Teena's gender than what he was reporting. When Lotter and Nissen realized they had been reported, they went after Teena again. They shot and killed him and two witnesses. At the time, transgender issues and hate crimes were not as well known to the general public (the victim was typically referred to as "she" and "her" in initial reporting), and this helped bring it out into the open. Both of Teena's killers were found guilty, and there was lobbying for more understanding of transphobia and for increased hate crime legislation. Several years later, a documentary called *The Brandon Teena Story* spread more awareness about what happened, and in 1999, Hilary Swank starred in a movie based on the case called *Boys Don't Cry*.

assaulted a white man with mental disabilities, putting a spotlight on this issue. The authorities believed the man was chosen both for being white and for having a disability. Video of the assault was posted online and went viral, making it easy for police to find the alleged culprits.

INTERSECTING IDENTITIES

Hate crimes are categorized, but many people can fall into more than one category. Sometimes, this makes them more or less likely to be the victim of a hate crime. For instance, a Native American transgender woman can experience racism, sexism, and transphobia, all rolled into one. There can also be difficulty in discussing hate crimes like Islamophobia or anti-Semitism because they can potentially branch into both religious and racial bias.

CHAPTER THREE

HATE CRIMES FROM HISTORY UNTIL NOW

O ftentimes, people who commit hate crimes grew up in poverty, and it's not unheard of to see a background of child abuse. A person taught abuse at home and lacking proper access to education and work is more likely to feel hatred for another person that may spiral into illegal, violent behavior.

Hate crimes can also spike as a result on what's going on in the world. If a person from a specific group commits a crime that is widely reported in the news, we might see other people in the same group more frequently attacked, even though they haven't done anything. Heated rhetoric can also cause a spike in hate crimes, like around election time. If a person lives within a society, group, or culture that encourages hatred toward another group or groups, this can normalize the hatred and encourage more people toward violence against other groups.

HATE CRIMES AROUND THE WORLD

As you travel the world, you will find more instances of hate, and different countries handle hate crimes in different ways. Depending on the country, the people most likely targeted for hate crimes can also change, reflecting the area's cultural shifts, hierarchy systems, and histories with prejudice. For instance, there aren't many hate crimes committed against Romani in America, but it's a serious issue being discussed in Europe. Christians experience a small percentage of American hate crimes, but they are sought out

Some of President Donald Trump's statements, like his interest in banning Muslims, have been seen by anti-hate crime groups as controversial and the sort of rhetoric that inflames violence.

and harassed for their religion in parts of the Middle East. Other prejudices seen in America are also prevalent around the globe, especially in regards to anti-Semitic and anti-LGBT hate crimes.

Hate crimes can be taken to extremes, like the genocides in Rwanda in 1994, where members of the Hutu ethnic group tried to eradicate another group, the Tutsi, or Darfur in 2007, where non-Arabs in the country were sought out and killed. The United States is not the only country to have hate crime laws, but in the majority of the world these crimes are treated like any other and not categorized in their own group.

Skulls serve as a reminder of what happened during the Rwandan genocide, when an estimated eight hundred thousand Tutsis were killed in a matter of months.

HATE GROUPS AND INDIVIDUALS

Hate groups are dedicated to hatred of groups, and they exist both on the right and left spectrum of politics. The Southern Poverty Law Center (SPLC) reported that radical right hate groups grew 14 percent in 2015. Groups like the Ku Klux Klan used to have more power than they do today, but they never really went away, and from 2014 to 2015 they went from having 72 chapters to 190. Neo-Nazis became more prevalent during the 2016 election, declaring that with recent politics from the alt-right that they were becoming mainstream. The alt-right refers to "alternative right," a far-right group that typically includes racism and white nationalism.

Looking to the far left, the SPLC noted a major increase in black separatist groups, going from 113 in 2014 to 180 in 2015. The organization said this growth was driven by anger about how black people are treated, but instead of attempting to fix this in productive ways, these separatist groups, like the New Black Panther Party (not to be confused with the Black Panther Party, which is different) want to spread prejudice instead. Black separatist groups are known to hate all white people, gay people, and especially Jews.

These hate groups fan the flames of hate, but not everyone in them breaks the law or commits a hate crime. People who have no affiliation or knowledge of hate groups can just as easily attack someone for being different.

MATTHEW SHEPARD

On October 6, 1998, twenty-one-year-old Matthew Shepard caught a ride with Aaron McKinney and Russell Henderson, two twenty-somethings he had met at a bar. McKinney and Henderson pistol-whipped him, beat him, and tied him to a fence alongside the road. They took his shoes so that if he managed to untie himself, he wouldn't be able to easily get away. Eighteen hours passed before anyone discovered Shepard, and by then it was too late to save his life. He was taken to the hospital but died several days later. The news story quickly exploded, in part because of the violence and in part because of Shepard's sexual orientation. Among activists and the media there were arguments that Shepard had been picked for murder because he was gay, and also arguments saying that was not the case. In response, President Bill Clinton called for the Hate Crimes Prevention Act to be approved by Congress. Both McKinney and Henderson were found guilty of the death of Shepard, and while the perpetrators sometimes gave contradictory testimony, McKinney eventually said in an interview for *Laramie Ten Years Later*, "Matt Shepard needed killing" and "The night I did it, I did have hatred for homosexuals." Because of all this, Matthew Shepard became one of the most well-known victims of hate crime cases, and lobbying after his death led to the 2009 Matthew Shepard and James Byrd, Jr., Hate Crimes Prevention Act, which included the categories of sexual orientation, gender identity, and disability for hate crime legislation. His mother, Judy Shepard, also founded the Matthew Shepard Foundation in his honor, which aims to fight hate crimes and support LGBT rights.

WHO IS COMMITTING HATE CRIMES?

There is more information out there on victims of hate crimes as opposed to perpetrators. Sometimes the perpetrators are never caught. The FBI keeps track of hate crime offenders, so let's look at a year's example. For 2015, there were 5,493 known offenders in 5,850 bias-motivated incidents. They recorded the age for 3,331 of the perpetrators, and 2,823 hate crimes were committed by grownups, and the other 508 hate crimes were committed by people under the age of eighteen.

In 2013, the Uniform Crime Reporting (UCR) Program also began keeping track of the race and ethnicity of people committing hate crimes. For 2015, it broke down like this: 48.4 percent were white, 24.3 percent were black, 9.1 percent "were groups made up of individuals of various races (group of multiple races)." One percent were Asian, while American Indian or Alaska Native and Native Hawaiian or Pacific Islander each came in with under 1 percent. A little over 16 percent are unknown.

CHALLENGES TO GETTING HATE CRIME NUMBERS

The FBI investigates and keeps careful track of hate crimes, operating with state, local, tribal, and federal authorities for their numbers. However, their numbers do not reflect the exact number of hate crimes.

Some hate crime victims do not report, and there are different reasons for this. Victims might fear what will happen to them if they report, they might not realize what happened to them was a hate crime, or they might simply be unable to report. A person might also be scared to report because they believe they were somehow to blame for the hate crime committed against them. For instance, they might feel they were in an area they shouldn't be, and the hate crime was committed there, so they don't want to tell. But the only one who committed a crime was the person who committed the hate crime, so a victim should not feel scared or embarrassed to go forward.

In some years, the FBI believes that as many as 70 percent of hate crimes go unreported. It's impossible to pin down the exact number, but it's clear that the number of hate crimes that happen is higher than what has been reported.

ARE HATE CRIMES GROWING IN AMERICA?

The new list of hate crime statistics from the FBI comes out at the end of each year with numbers for the previous year, so it can be difficult to gauge the number of hate crimes until after the previous year has been over for a while.

After the 2016 presidential election, the media began to report on an upswing in hate crimes, with many looking toward then president-elect Donald

JAMES BYRD JR.

In 1998, James Byrd Jr. was an African American Texan who was picked up by several white supremacists. First the men beat Byrd, and then they chained him to the back of their truck. Being dragged behind the truck caused his body to break into pieces, and investigators discovered body parts in seventy-five different spots along the road. When the men were done driving, they tossed what was left of his body into a black cemetery. The perpetrators were later arrested and found guilty, while the country was struck by the savagery of Byrd's murder. Almost immediately it became a famous case and it led to changes in hate crime laws. Three years later, Governor Rick Perry of Texas expanded penalties for hate crimes committed in his state. Byrd's death also led to the Matthew Shepard and James Byrd, Jr., Hate Crimes Prevention Act of 2009, signed into law by President Barack Obama. But even death did not prevent Byrd from experiencing racially motivated hatred. The Ku Klux Klan marched through his town as a result of his murder, and his grave site was later desecrated.

Trump with accusations that he was encouraging, enabling, and normalizing hate crimes and not condemning them. People were reporting their bias-based experiences to the Southern Poverty Law Center, which was keeping track. During the time of November 9 to December 12, 2016, the SPLC reported 1,094 bias-related incidents. To put that in perspective, that was about one-seventh the total number of hate crimes victims reported by the FBI for the entire year before, but this happened in just over a month. At the same time, it's important to note that these were all hate incidents and not necessarily hate crimes (meaning not illegal) and while the SPLC worked on confirmation, they acknowledged some of the incidents were anecdotal. This means they have not been fully investigated and cannot be fully confirmed or denied.

Swastikas, the main symbol of Nazism, and the letters "KKK" for "Klu Klux Klan," have been spray-painted on this Maine synagogue.

In March 2017, the nonpartisan Center for the Study of Hate & Extremism from California State University, San Bernardino, released a study saying they saw hate crimes increase more than 20 percent in selected cities after the 2016 election. They got these numbers by studying data collected from nine cities' police departments.

CHAPTER FOUR

HATE CRIMES AND THE LAW

Hate crime laws have changed over the years, and we'll probably see more changes as time goes by. Over the years, some legal milestones have taken place.

THE CIVIL RIGHTS ACT

The Civil Rights Act of 1968, while existing before the term "hate crime" was around, essentially dealt with hate crimes committed against people because of their skin color, religious beliefs, or where they were from, but it concentrated on a specific kind of discrimination: preventing people from doing things like going to school or getting a job. The United States Department of Justice explains, "In 1968, Congress also made it a crime to use, or threaten to use, force to interfere with housing rights because of the victim's race, color, religion, sex, or national origin; in 1988, protections on the basis of familial status and were added."

More laws came into effect in 1996, with the Church Arson Prevention Act. Because many hate crimes are done against property, including property for religious purposes, it became illegal, according to the Department of Justice, to "deface, damage, or destroy religious real property, or interfere with a person's religious practice, in situations affecting interstate commerce. The Act also bars defacing, damaging, or destroying religious property because of the race, color, or ethnicity of persons associated with the property."

Then-president Bill Clinton spoke to Senator Carol Moseley-Braun in 1996, just after passing the bipartisan Church Arson Prevention Act.

THE MATTHEW SHEPARD AND JAMES BYRD, JR., HATE CRIMES PREVENTION ACT

Other groups that experienced hate-based violence lobbied to be included for protections as well. For instance, if a person was the victim of a hate crime because of their sexual orientation, gender, gender identity, or disability, this was not seen as a hate crime by the federal government, even though a significant number of hate crimes are committed against people in these groups.

This altered in 2009, with the Matthew Shepard and James Byrd, Jr., Hate Crimes Prevention Act, which worked on the federal level (meaning it affected all states) and it included these categories. Named after two famous victims of hate crimes, this law was a major breakthrough for hate crime law.

The Justice Department explains, "The Shepard-Byrd Act makes it a federal crime to willfully cause bodily injury, or attempt to do so using a dangerous weapon, because of the victim's actual or perceived race, color, religion, or national origin. The Act also extends federal hate crime prohibitions to crimes committed because of the actual or perceived religion, national origin, gender, sexual orientation, gender identity, or disability of any person, only where the crime affected interstate or foreign commerce or occurred within federal special maritime and territorial jurisdiction. The Shepard-Byrd Act is the first statute allowing federal criminal prosecution of hate crimes motivated by the victim's actual or perceived sexual orientation or gender identity."

The act received a lot of attention as it was being debated by elected officials. In the House, 249 people approved it, while 175 voted against it. It then moved on to the Senate, where it passed by a vote of 63–28.

Politicians who were against the act usually had a few main arguments. One was that it would hinder free speech, for example, if a religious leader spoke against gay people, but this was an inaccurate statement because of how hate crime legislation is set up. Another argument was that the law was unnecessary because state governments were already handling violent crimes.

Attorney General Eric Holder, a supporter of the act, disagreed with these arguments. Speaking in favor of the act, he said that action needed to be taken because "nearly one hate crime for every hour of every day over the span of a decade" had happened between the years 1998 to 2007.

DO HATE CRIME LAWS DETER HATE CRIMES?

Hate crime laws are put in place to punish people who commit crimes, and there is debate on whether or not they deter them. In other words, do fewer people commit hate crimes because they don't want to get in trouble? The same debate can be seen with the death penalty and other laws.

With hate crime legislation, there really is no easy way to measure, in part because so many hate crimes go unreported. Politicians and activists also have differing opinions, and until there is more information, reports, and research on hate crimes, it can be hard to say for certain.

SEAN KENNEDY

After her twenty-year-old son, Sean Kennedy, was killed in 2007, Elke Kennedy began lobbying for new hate crime legislation. Speaking to CNN, Elke described how Sean was walking away from a bar when eighteen-year-old Stephen Andrew Moller "walked over to Sean and called him a faggot and punched him in the face." Moller then left a message on the cell phone of one of Sean's acquaintances: "You tell your faggot friend when he wakes up he owes me 500 dollars for my broken hand." One punch was all it took, since it caused Kennedy's brain and brain stem to separate. He was pronounced brain dead within a day. Because of the way hate crime laws were at the time, this did not count as a hate crime in South Carolina, and Moller was found guilty of involuntary manslaughter and was sentenced to being in the country lockup for 199 days and then sent to prison for one year. Elke Kennedy felt that because her son was sought out for being gay, this should have counted as

Elke Kennedy and her husband, James Parker, are standing at a candlelight vigil for Sean Kennedy on February 10, 2009.

a hate crime and Moller should have received a harsher sentence. As a result, she lobbied across the country. When new federal hate crime legislation went through in 2009, she told CNN, "This is a huge milestone, but it is not the end of the fight. We have to change the hearts and minds."

ARGUMENTS AGAINST THE IDEA OF HATE CRIME LAWS

Not everyone supports hate crime laws the way they are. Some racist groups or activists downplay hate crimes or hate crime laws to further their own gains. At the same time, there are people who are concerned about fighting hate but feel that hate crimes are not the way to go about it. One argument is that punishing hate crimes, as opposed to teaching tolerance instead, causes more anger among groups and does not prevent future hate crimes from happening. Speaking along these lines, Flor Bermudez of the Transgender Law Center spoke critically of hate crime laws while championing equal rights, telling CNN, "Hate crime laws do nothing to ensure the safety of transgender people, since they don't address the root cause of the problem. To the contrary, hate crime laws use criminalization and enhanced punishment in a way that ultimately only expand the criminal system that already disproportionately targets transgender women of color."

There is also the argument that the motive for a crime shouldn't matter in sentencing because a crime is a crime, and all crimes involve some level of hate. In the court of law, however, motive often does count in sentencing, whether the crime being discussed is a hate crime or not.

Some people also contend that the term "hate crime" is overused and is more about getting pity than fighting hate. Instead of actually fighting hate, they argue, it encourages people to feel victimized and gets communities stirred up.

Sometimes, people are also critical of hate crime laws but their understanding of a hate crime law is not quite accurate. A common argument is that hate crime laws violate free speech and free thought, but because free speech and thought are protected in America, this is not the case. Another misconception is that it's always considered a hate crime if a group that's not considered marginalized does something illegal to a group that's considered marginalized. For instance, there is a misconception that if a white person attacks a black person, the law will consider it a hate crime and punish the white person more than it would if the perpetrator had attacked another white person. Because hate crimes are about the motive, and motive must be proven in the court of law, this is not accurate. In the aforementioned example, the white person would have had to attack the black person simply because they were black for it to be a hate crime. If a person is attacked for any other reason, like robbery, and there's no racial bias involved, it will involve other charges.

INTERVIEW WITH JUDY SHEPARD, FOUNDING PRESIDENT OF THE MATTHEW SHEPARD FOUNDATION BOARD OF DIRECTORS

How are state hate crime laws different from federal law?
It differs from state to state. Five states [Arkansas, Indiana, South Carolina, Utah, and Wyoming] do not have hate crime laws. Some states have hate crime laws that do not cover sexual orientation or gender identity, or they cover one or the other, but not both. Some states have laws that are all-inclusive. It's very much a patchwork nationwide, which is really why the federal law was so important.

What happens if you're a victim of a nonviolent hate crime in a state without hate crime laws?
Unless there's a separate law that would cover the harassment, it's not a question that has a good answer.

Why do you think the state laws vary so much?
Some states are reluctant, in my opinion, to regard the LGBT community as a protected class, even though federally they are. It's personal philosophy of the constituents or the voters or whatever they think that is. Because each state has the right to do some of their own laws, they're going to vary based on the culture, the religion, the makeup of the state.

How can people find out the laws in their own state?
They can check out the statues for the state laws. Any library is going to have that. Or they can contact their representatives from their area, or even a local law enforcement agency.

(continued on the next page)

(continued from the previous page)

If someone wants to give their opinion to their state on local hate crime laws, how would you recommend they go about that?

Letters, calls, visits to their area representative. If you're not their constituent, you're not going to have as much influence. But it's still some influence, because volume of inquiries matter. They pay attention to that.

What would activists like yourself like to see for hate crime laws in the future?

They need to be uniform, for one thing. I understand that states are going to differ, but reporting of hate crimes is really the most difficult part right now. Because if you live in a state where you can still be fired from your job for being gay, you're not going to report a hate crime that happened to you based on your orientation because you might lose your job. It takes a long time to prosecute these cases, and it takes so much energy to get them done that many of them give up. It's a difficult process, and it needs to be made more understandable and easier to execute.

Senators Gordon Smith and Ted Kennedy, who introduced the Local Law Enforcement Hate Crimes Prevention Act, stand with Judy Shepard at a press conference.

STATE LAWS

Even with this federal legislation, each state has its own ways of dealing with hate crimes, which can make things confusing. The Matthew Shepard Act only covers violent hate crimes federally, so if a state without hate crime legislation has something like a vandalism case, it would not be covered by this act and wouldn't be prosecuted as a hate crime. South Carolina, where Dylann Roof killed people in church, does not have hate crime laws, but because it was a violent act, the federal government got involved. Nonviolent but harmful hate crimes in states without hate crime laws often fall through the cracks and there isn't much information on them.

CHAPTER FIVE

TAKING ACTION ON HATE CRIMES

Hate crimes are an upsetting subject and learning about them or experiencing them can make many people feel angry, sad, or scared. Young people can take action on this subject, doing everything from talking to their elected representatives about their own opinions on hate crime laws to working to prevent hate crimes. While hate crimes are upsetting, there are many people who dedicate their lives to stopping hate, so it's easy to find allies and activists.

EDUCATION

One of the biggest keys toward preventing hate crimes is education. This often includes education on tolerance and different people's cultures and identities. Sometimes clashes or misunderstandings arise from cultural or religious differences, and this education can show how to navigate these areas without hate or violence being involved. Even communities that have long histories of hostility toward one another have found ways to get along and work together.

The internet can be a great way for people to find out information on hate crimes and their prevention, but remember to always check sources and double-check facts.

If your school doesn't have this sort of education, you can talk with your teachers or principal, or with a foundation dedicated to fighting hate crimes. You might be able to introduce tolerance education to your school. The Department of Justice has its own manual, called *Preventing Youth Hate Crime,* that schools and communities can use to talk about hate crimes with young people. The manual is available for free on its website, is twenty-five pages long, and includes information, resources, and contact details.

INTERVIEW WITH MICHAEL LIEBERMAN, DIRECTOR OF THE CIVIL RIGHTS POLICY PLANNING CENTER AT THE ANTI-DEFAMATION LEAGUE

What do you think are some of the best ways people can take action in regards to hate crimes?
We as communities need to take them seriously. There are no trivial acts of anti-Semitism, no trivial acts of Islamophobia, no trivial acts of homophobia. We must demand that our public officials and law enforcement officials also treat them seriously. I think it's critically important that communities rally around victims of hate violence. If there's a mosque that is vandalized, it's important that not only Muslims show up for the cleanup, but there's a community response. If there's a bomb threat to a JCC [Jewish Community Center] or day school, it's reinforcing of community values if the minister from the Presbyterian Church and the priest from the local parish also show up. These crimes are message crimes, and one way to demonstrate that the message of bias is rejected is to show up, stand up, stand out. Send a message right back that we reject this bigotry.

What sort of education do you recommend to help prevent hate crimes?
The ADL drafted the first hate crime law in 1981; now the federal government, the District of Columbia and forty-five states have hate crime laws. But it's so much better to prevent these crimes from happening in the first place, and that starts from education. It's a serious effort

to train students in anti-bias awareness and what it means to be an ally for someone who is targeted for their difference. There is evidence, science, and research that people who are bullies and people who are bullied sometimes are also involved in more serious activities later, crossing the line from hatred and bias into actual hate crimes.

Why do you believe hate crime laws serve as a deterrent?
I believe the most important evidence is the support from law enforcement officials. Obviously groups like the Human Rights Campaign or the NAACP or the Anti-Defamation League are going to support strong hate crime laws because we are the victims of these hate crimes. But police organizations are not really known as touchy-feely types; the reason that every major law enforcement organization in the country supports hate crime laws is because they think it will have an impact preventing and deterring hate crimes.

Do you have any other advice on preventing hate crimes?
The vast majority of hate crimes occur between people who do not know each other and the perpetrator selects the victim because of difference. If we can teach kids from a young age not to be fearful on the basis of that difference, but to respect and learn about that difference, then I think we can have a real chance of diminishing the number of hate crimes in the future.

LEARNING TO RECOGNIZE HATE

Many people who support hate crime laws will say that the laws help the issue, but the only way to truly tackle the issue for good is to get to the root of it. This includes educating yourself on hate and how hate can manifest. Looking through history and at different cultures can show that hate manifests itself in similar but different ways. It is also important to better understand the perpetrators and why they felt a need to do what they did, because this can help in preventing future violent hate crimes.

GETTING INVOLVED WITH GROUPS THAT FIGHT HATE CRIMES

Many groups fight hate crimes, like tracking them and getting the community involved in reporting, education, and tolerance. Some of the biggest foundations fighting hate crimes include the Southern Poverty Law Center, the Anti-Defamation League, and the Matthew Shepard Foundation.

By visiting these websites, you can learn more about hate crimes, what each foundation does, and how you can take part. These foundations are usually interested in receiving volunteers or donations, and they can also help bring hate crime education to your school. Many of them have social media channels as well, giving people an easy way to learn more and access news and updates.

The Southern Poverty Law Center is headquartered in Montgomery, Alabama, but you can find groups fighting hate crimes around the country.

REPORTING INCIDENTS

If you or someone you know may be the victim of a hate crime, it's important to report to the authorities. Many people don't report out of fear or because they don't understand it's something they can report. People who are afraid of reporting should let the police know this because the police can make sure they're protected.

It's important to contact law enforcement, but you can also get additional help from one of the various hate crime prevention foundations. In order to help fight hate

If you think you may be the victim of a hate crime, it's important to speak up to keep yourself safe and to keep others safe.

crimes, authorities need to know when hate crimes happen. Some foundations dedicated to fighting hate crimes can also help you report if you're scared. They have experience on the topic and know how the laws work. So if you reach out to the appropriate foundation, it can help you through this and give you support.

After the 2016 election, many magazines and websites, especially those aimed for young people, began asking their readers to report their experiences with hate crimes. This can help spread awareness, too, but the most important people to report to are the police. When it comes to hate crimes, it's important to know that you are not alone.

10 GREAT QUESTIONS TO ASK A CIVIL RIGHTS LAWYER

1. How are hate crimes different from other crimes?
2. What do you recommend a person do if he or she sees a potential hate crime happening?
3. Why do you think there's a need to categorize hate crimes in their own categories?
4. What are the best ways to fight hate crimes?
5. What are the best ways to get to the root of why hate crimes happen?
6. How can we encourage more people to report hate crimes?
7. How can young people take action on hate crimes?
8. What are good ways to dispel myths and misinformation about hate crimes?
9. How can we work to fight hate, while still respecting freedom of speech and people who might disagree?
10. What do you see happening in the future of hate crime legislation?

anti-Semitism Prejudice and discrimination against Jewish people.

bias A feeling against something that is often preconceived.

ethnicity A group of people within a certain culture that shares multiple traits.

federal Relating to the central government (as opposed to state governments).

genocide Purposefully killing off an entire group of people because of the group they're in.

homophobia Hatred and fear of gay people.

ideology A series of thoughts and beliefs a person can have about things like the world and human cultures.

institutional racism Where people are treated unequally because of their race by the social institutions in their midst. There are other examples of this, like institutional sexism.

Islamophobia Prejudice and fear against Muslims.

LGBT Lesbian, gay, bisexual, and transgender.

marginalized Having limited power.

oppression Having unfair and cruel power over someone.

persecution Making someone suffer, usually for being different.

rhetoric A type of talking a person uses, sometimes used to persuade people to his or her beliefs.

Romani An ethnic group, also known as Gypsies, that

has experienced a lot of discrimination in Europe.

sexual orientation One's preference in the sex of their intimate partners.

Sikh A member of the Sikh religion, a monotheistic faith that started in the 1500s.

synagogue A house of worship for Jewish people.

transgender Refers to a person whose gender identity does not fit with the gender that the person was assigned at birth.

transphobia Fear and prejudice against transgender people.

white supremacist A person who believes white people are superior to all others.

Anti-Defamation League
605 Third Avenue
New York, NY 10158
(212) 885-7700
Website: http://www.adl.org
Facebook: @anti.defamation.league/
Twitter: @ADL_National
Instagram: @adl_national/
Founded more than one hundred years ago, the ADL
    fights all forms of hate crimes and bias, with a con-
    centration on anti-Semitism.

Canadian Civil Liberties Association
90 Eglinton Avenue E Suite 900
Toronto, ON M4P 2Y3
Canada
(416) 363-0321
Website: http://www.ccla.org
Facebook: @cancivlib
Twitter: @cancivlib
CCLA works as a nonprofit for Canadian civil rights.

Human Rights First
75 Broad Street, 31st Floor
New York, NY 10004
(202) 370-3323
Website: http://www.humanrightsfirst.org
Facebook: @humanrightsfirst

Twitter: @humanrights1st
Human Rights First is an American-based international
    human rights organization.

Matthew Shepard Foundation
800 18th Street, Suite 101
Denver, CO 80202
(303) 830-7400
Website: http://www.matthewshepard.org
Facebook: @MatthewShepardFoundation/
Twitter: @mattshepardfdn
Instagram: @mattshepardfdn
Judy and Dennis Shepard founded this organization
    after the death of their son, Matthew. The organiza-
    tion fights hate and bigotry, with a concentration on
    LGBT issues.

Southern Poverty Law Center
400 Washington Avenue
Montgomery, AL 36104
(888) 414-7752
Website: http://www.splcenter.org
Facebook: @SPLCenter
Twitter: @splcenter
Instagram: @splcenter
The SPLC is a legal advocacy group that monitors hate
    groups and has a concentration on civil rights.

Stop Racism and Hate Canada
324280 Nelson Street
Vancouver, BC V6B 2E2

Canada
Website: http://www.stopracism.ca
Stop Racism and Hate Canada has a place on its website where Canadians can report hate crimes.

WEBSITES

Because of the changing nature of internet links, Rosen Publishing has developed an online list of websites related to the subject of this book. This site is updated regularly. Please use this link to access the list:

http://www.rosenlinks.com/NTKL/Hate

FOR FURTHER READING

Aaronson, Ely. *From Slave Abuse to Hate Crime.* Cambridge, UK: Cambridge University Press, 2014.

Abramovitz, Melissa. *Hate Crimes in America.* 3rd ed. Minneapolis MN: Essential Library, 2016.

Chahal, Kusminder. *Supporting Victims of Hate Crime.* Bristol, UK: Policy Press, 2017.

Gerstenfeld, Phyllis B. *Hate Crimes: Causes, Controls, and Controversies.* Thousand Oaks, CA: Sage Publications, 2017.

Hand, Carol. *Everything You Need to Know About Sexism* (The Need to Know Library). New York, NY: Rosen Publishing, 2018.

Lombardo, Jennifer. *Hate Crimes: When Intolerance Turns Violent.* Farmington Hills, MI: Lucent Press, 2017.

Newton, Michael. *Hate Crime in America, 1968–2013.* Jefferson, NC: McFarland, 2014.

Pezella, Frank S. *Hate Crime Statutes.* New York, NY: Springer, 2017.

Timmons, Angie. *Everything You Need to Know About Racism* (The Need to Know Library). New York, NY: Rosen Publishing, 2018.

Turpin-Petrosino, Carolyn. *Understanding Hate Crimes.* Abingdon-on-Thames, UK: Routledge, 2015.

Associated Press. "10 Years Later, Dragging Death
    Changes Town." NBC News. June 2008. http://www
    .nbcnews.com/id/25008925/ns/us_newslife/t
    /yearslaterdraggingdeathchangestown/#
    .WNmHT7gdCNh.
Borden, Jeremy. "From Victims' Families, Forgiveness for
    Accused Charleston Gunman Dylann Roof." Washing-
    ton Post. June 2015. https://www.washingtonpost.com
    /politics/southcarolinagovernorurgesdeathpenalty
    chargesinchurchslayings/2015/06/19/3c03972216781
    1e59ddce3353542100c_story.html?utm_term
    =.a36f625e3afe.
Buchanan, Susie. "Violence Against American Indians is
    a Pervasive Problem." Southern Poverty Law Center.
    January 2007. https://www.splcenter.org/fightinghate
    /intelligencereport/2007/violenceagainstamerican
    indianspervasiveproblem.
CNN. "Two Years After Son's Death, Mother Finds Solace
    in Hate Crimes Bill." October 2009. http://www.cnn
    .com/2009/CRIME/10/28/hate.crime.bill.mother/index
    .html?iref=24hours.
Coleman, Kora. "Texas Executes White Supremacist
    Convicted of Racially Motivated Murder." NPR.
    September 2011. http://www.npr.org/sections
    /thetwoway/2011/09/21/140666067/texassetto
    executenotoriousmurderer.
Fairyington, Stephanie. "Two Decades After Brandon
    Teena's Murder, a Look Back at Falls City." Atlantic.
    December 2013. https://www.theatlantic.com

/national/archive/2013/12/twodecadesafterbrandon
teenasmurderalookbackatfallscity/282738.

Frieden, Terry. "Holder Pushes for HateCrimes Law; GOP
Unpersuaded." CNN. January 2009. http://www.cnn
.com/2009/POLITICS/06/25/holder.hate.crimes/index
.html?iref=24hours.

Grinberg, Emanuella. "Transgender Hate Crime Guilty
Plea in Federal Court Is a First." CNN. December
2016. http://www.cnn.com/2016/12/22/politics
/mississippitransgenderhatecrime.

Moore, John. "Murderer: 'Matt Shepard needed killing.'"
Denver Post. October 2009. http://www.denverpost
.com/2009/10/01/murderermattshepardneededkilling.

Potok, Mark. "The Year in Hate and Extremism." Southern
Poverty Law Center. February 2016. https://www
.splcenter.org/fightinghate/intelligencereport/2016
/yearhateandextremism.

Smith, Grant. "U.S. Hate Crimes Up 20 Percent in
2016 Fueled by Election CampaignReport." Reuters.
March 2017. https://www.yahoo.com/news
/uhatecrimes20percent2016fueledelection031944099
.html?soc_src=mail&soc_trk=ma.

Southern Poverty Law Center. "Update: 1,094 BiasRelated
Incidents in the Month Following the Election." December 2016. https://www.splcenter.org/hatewatch/2016
/12/16/update1094biasrelatedincidentsmonthfollowing
election.

United States Department of Justice. "The Matthew Shepard and James Byrd, Jr., Hate Crimes Prevention Act
of 2009." August 2016. https://www.justice.gov/crt
/matthewshepardandjamesbyrdjrhatecrimes
preventionact20090.

ABOUT THE AUTHOR

Danica Davidson has a background in journalism, often covering current social issues for young people, including the topic of hate crimes. She is also the author of children's novels and comic books.

PHOTO CREDITS

Cover Joe Raedle/Getty Images; back cover Photo by Marianna armata/Moment/Getty Images; p. 5 Jessica Kourkounis/Getty Images; pp. 6, 18, 27, 36, 46 irisphoto1/Shutterstock.com; p. 7 Charlotte Observer/Tribune News Service/Getty Images; pp. 10–11 Sean Rayford/Getty Images; pp. 14–15 National Geographic Creative/Bridgeman Images; p. 19 Underwood Archives/Archive Photos/Getty Images; p. 22 Robert Nickelsberg/Getty Images; p. 24 Mario Tama/Getty Images; p. 28 Evan El-Amin/Shutterstock.com; p. 29 Gideon Mendel/Corbis Historical/Getty Images; pp. 35, 37, 40 © AP Images; p. 44 Chip Somodevilla/Getty Images; p. 47 Syda Productions/Shutterstock.com; p. 51 Philip Scalia/Alamy Stock Photo; p. 52 © iStockphoto.com/MachineHeadz.

Design: Michael Moy; Layout: Tahara Anderson; Editor: Bethany Bryan; Photo Researcher: Sherri Jackson